BOB MARLEY
SOUL REBEL-NATURAL MYSTIC

ADRIAN BOOT/ VIVIEN GOLDMAN

ST. MARTIN'S PRESS
NEW YORK

An Eel Pie Publishing Ltd./Bellow & Higton book
in association with The Hutchinson Publishing Group Ltd.
First published in 1981 by The Hutchinson Publishing Group Ltd.,
17-21, Conway Street, London WIP 6PS.

Copyright © 1982 by Adrian Boot/Vivien Goldman
For information, write: St. Martin's Press,
175 Fifth Avenue, New York, N.Y. 10010
Manufactured in the United States of America

Library of Congress Cataloging in Publication Data

Goldman, Vivien.
  Bob Marley, soul rebel—natural mystic.

  1. Marley, Bob.   2. Musicians, Black—Jamaica—
Biography.   I. Title.
ML410.M344G6   784.5'5'00924 [B]   81-14598
ISBN 0-312-08727-6 (pbk.)   AACR2

Printed in the U.S.A.

Special thanks:
Rob Partridge
Neil Spencer
Lynne Boot
Kate Simon
Roz Reines

All photographs by Adrian Boot, except where otherwise credited.
All song lyrics © Rondor Music 1981, reproduced by permission —
except 'Small Axe', 'Mr. Brown', 'Slave Driver', 'Sun Is Shinning',
'Do It Twice' and 'She's Gone', which are © Leosong 1981,
reproduced by permission.

THE HON. ROBERT NESTA MARLEY O.M.
(Bob Marley-Berhane Selassie)
6th February 1945-11th May 1981

How long must they kill our prophets
While we stand aside and look?
Some say it's just a part of it –
We've got to fulfill the book . . .
('Redemption Song': **Uprising**)

He was always billed as 'the Trenchtown Experience', and people that checked for Bob Marley thought of him first as a ghetto youth. As if you couldn't think of him without a backdrop of steaming zinc shacks about to burst into apocalyptic blaze, burning all pollution tonight.

But this urban guerrilla really comes from the country, from St. Anns, the market town that slopes down to the sea, with an Edwardian clocktower that brings back Brighton. His white British naval officer father was gone before Bob was born, an Aquarian and a Joseph (of the Rastafarian Twelve Tribes Of Israel), on February 6, 1945. He grew up in the country, riding donkeys, milking cows and goats, swimming in the streams and the sea. He used to enjoy going out tracking birds with his sling-shot, and at night, when the sun had switched off cleanly as an electric light, and the neon green of the hills had dampened down to blue, Marley could listen to the night insects screech and coo at each other in their jagged off-beat cross-rhythms. If the life of an international reggae superstar had begun to pall, Marley would have liked to be a farmer again.

"Isn't it a nice feeling . . . isn't it a nice day. Isn't it a *nice* feeling. . . ." Bob Marley is scat singing, improvising with his old boho acoustic guitar. The Wailers are on the road in Europe in 1977, promoting **Exodus**, the album that springboarded Marley to international star status with disco hits like 'Jamming' and 'Exodus'. For weeks the Wailers convoy, complete with ital (vegetarian, salt-free Rasta food) cook have been clambering into buses and disgorging into alien amphitheatres, collapsing into no-number hotel rooms. Today is the day off, finally, and this translucent afternoon has an added bonus – the sound of a river that almost drowns out the cars double-parking outside the Munich Hilton.

All round the room, Wailers and friends are singing along, making it up as they go, clattering counter-rhythms on tables and chair legs, clanking the fork against the silver salt cellar. The sort of spontaneous singalong you'd expect round a camp-fire under the sky, not in the seal-grey and beige neutrality of this Hilton hotel.

Look at Marley now. Something about the way he weaves the mood, draws the music out and round, is a reminder that so many of his songs about power, personal, spiritual, political or perhaps magical, are spin-offs of his soul. Right now, it shines in his face; he is the Soul Rebel, the Natural Mystic, and the Duppy (Ghost) Conqueror.

Marley knew about the Shining, before that name for mystic communication was popularised. As his dreadlocks grew, they thundered over his shoulders. Short, slight, compact, his body seemed a slender lightning conductor for so much rushing energy. Picture those locks as antennae for supernatural messages, as the Rastas understood them, and you can see why Bob Marley was such a strong transmitter, one country boy who took a little local Caribbean island music and thrashed the world's music with it. Not just by penetrating rock charts where no rebellious black face was usually seen, but by percolating the reggae rhythms through, bubble by bubble, till the music had thoroughly soaked the subconscious of people of all races, in many places.

More than that, he popularised that Molotov mix, revolution and religion. Marley's consciousness grew, and his music moved from early 60's covers of 'What's New Pussycat' and 'I Want To Hold Your Hand' to rhythms of resistance and African chants. He stopped hankering after smooth threads, machete-crease trousers, looking so neat in his mohair suit. He gave up the gold lamé Beatle jackets and discovered African daishikis. By the time Marley became known outside Jamaica, in the early 70's, his Black Power style Afro had begun to corkscrew-curl in a different fashion, into the dreadlocks that were the outward sign of his devotion to Rastafari.

Rastas believe that Emperor Haile Selassie of Ethiopia – Jah Rastafari (literally translated: lion's head) – is the living God. Innumerable times, Marley was asked by interviewers how he, a supposed radical revolutionary, could hold divine a despot who left his people starving while he counted his numbered Swiss bank accounts? How he could claim Jah was alive when Selassie was visibly dead?

The words were scarcely an irritant to Marley after a while; his own direct experience, his being, fed him different information from the questions posed by these 'crazy baldheads'. "Dese newspapers don' understand, or they want to crush my thinking into the dust," he told American journalist Tim White; and confirming the intensity of his vision, he told British journalist Neil Spencer, "Y'know, Jah appear to me in a vision – and every time he look just a bit older than me. 'Im don't look ninety year old or anything. Like, if I'm thirty, (which Marley was at the time of this interview in '75) then 'Im look about thirty-five. Man, it's so sweet; it's me brother, me father, me mother, me creator, everything. . . ." But Marley never gave up attempting to explain his beliefs.

Rastas yearn to return to Africa – some practically, some theoretically. They structure their views round the Bible, and are supposed to read a chapter a day. Like all Bible-based religions, Rasta provides strict codes about relations between the sexes – menstruating women are not only untouchable, they're also not supposed to prepare food, for example. It seems disgusting and oppressive to non-Rasta women, but a Dread woman looks on it cheerfully as time off domestic chores. They are Rasta women because that's how they find their sense of freedom and well-being. It may look like chains from the outside, but from inside it's a safety-belt.

Camera

Injunctions about not cutting your hair, covering your head, and strict dietary laws about not eating scavengers overlap with Judaism, and Marley belonged to an organisation called the Twelve Tribes of Israel. The basic back-to-Africa principles of Rastafari, promoted by a remarkable Jamaican called Marcus Garvey (also from St. Anns), reflect Zionism.

Rasta encourages the smoking of ganja (marijuana) as a help in two favourite Rasta pastimes, meditation and reasoning. It is a philosophical, almost Zen-passive faith, which puts it right in line with other religions as counter-revolutionary opiates of the people; except that Marley, a most sincere Rasta, found that his faith just helped him be more militant, when necessary. Rastas are the outlaws of Jamaican society – traditionally scoffed at as unclean 'Blackheart Men'. They have also produced some of Jamaica's finest arts. They do not believe in death. Rasta no go a burial.

Those dreadlocks fascinated the non-Rasta world. For the media, Marley was too seductive a package to ignore. Massive mystique. How does he ever get his hair to go like that, anyway? Is he *clean*? And how much pot did you say he smokes in one day? You mean his religion tells him to go and break the law like that? The sexual seal was set on his public image by Miss World of 1976 (Miss Jamaica, Cindy Breakspeare) acknowledging him as Her Man, despite his nine children by different women. Marley's presence infiltrated the blandest, most white-ass suburban record collections, and people that might never have questioned the authority of government were exposed to, fascinated by, the music of a true revolutionary who always knew himself as a humble farmer and ghetto child. A prophet, in the truest sense. *'Cos if you are the big tree, we are the small axe, aiming to cut you down, ready to cut you down. . . .* ('Small Axe')

Isn't it a nice feeling. On that triumphant European tour, the football injury bandage on Bob's foot didn't seem a serious thing. Marley, the health nut, restlessly sprinting from the studio to a game of soccer, twisting his whole body into a game of table football, playing on the attack – a few minor wounds and abrasions scarcely counted. Shock horror rumours spread that Bob's foot had gone bad somehow. There was talk of amputation, then a vast relief that it wasn't going to happen – that Bob would still be able to twirl like a dervish. But the reality was more sinister. Melanoma cancer, that was to send cells on a war dance round his liver and lungs, till he collapsed while jogging round Central Park after supporting the Commodores at New York's Madison Square Gardens.

In Marley's life-long process of international infiltration, America had remained stubborn. Bob had already been forced to cancel one American tour. *I don't want to wait in vain for your love,* Bob sang on **Exodus**, and it seemed to apply to more than the love of one woman. *Don't treat me like a puppet on a string, 'cos I know how to do my thing. Don't talk to me as if you think I'm dumb, I wanna know if you're gonna come. . . .* Bob's old singing partner, Bunny Wailer, had even written a song on the subject: *Get up you black yankees, don't be no follow fashion monkey,* all about black America's stubborn insistence on disco as the desirable form of contemporary black music. *It's your love that I'm waiting on – it's my love that you're running from. . . .* ('Wait In Vain')

Suddenly it seemed that love was about to be returned. Marley had played with Stevie Wonder, at Kingston's National Stadium, but now Wonder had recorded the ace-jivin' street-box-hoppin' sound of 1980's summer – 'Masterblaster'. Riffing around one of Marley's better known songs, 'Jamming', Wonder had eased Marley from his alien, disturbing slot in the American musical psyche to the position of a pal who might yet become a close friend.

This was not the first time that Marley's public profile had been polished up by fellow musicians. At a time when Marley's musical

Courtesy Island Records.

career had seemed very shaky after a series of rip-offs, it was Johnny Nash who stepped in, involving Bob in all manner of excitement, like unfinished film soundtracks in Sweden. Nash recorded a few Marley tunes – 'Stir It Up', 'Guava Jelly', 'Nice Time' – in 1972, giving Marley his first non-Jamaican hits as a writer, and the opportunity to record 'Reggae On Broadway' for CBS. In 1974 rock guitarist Eric Clapton covered 'I Shot The Sheriff'. Again, acceptance by an established star upped the wattage of Bob's public persona.

The natural progression of his increasing fame seemed inexorable, as if Marley's movie was rapidly spinning out into the classic Hollywood happy ending. But the plot took a downward twist in New York's Sloan Kettering Hospital, where intensive tests showed alarming results. Marley was rumoured to have retreated to Sheshamani (an area of the Rastas' Zion, Ethiopia, which is specially reserved for Dreads), for some spiritual upliftment, but in fact he went to the Sunshine House Cancer Clinic in Bad Wiesse, West Germany. There Dr. Josef Issels prescribed unorthodox treatments, involving ultra-violet rays, injections and special diets.

Issels had become a controversial figure, particularly over his treatment of Olympic athlete Lillian Board, but his remarkable success rate of 20% (all his patients have been diagnosed as incurable by conventional methods), was an inspiration for Marley, and apparently the two men struck up a warm friendship.

Marley told me of his views on death in an interview in '79:

VG: How come you're aware of the danger of being assassinated, when you say there's no such thing as death?

MARLEY: Hold on, now. You think you can go out there and lay down in front of the car and let it run over you? If I go outside and see the big bus coming and put my head underneath it, what do you think will happen?

VG: Your head will be crushed. And what will you be then?

MARLEY (shouts): DEAD! This is where people make a mistake. They say that the flesh doesn't value anything, but that's the biggest lie. This flesh is what you've got, what God put inside you is your life. That's the way I think, that's the way I'm organised, because I don't stray from my roots, and my roots is God. But sister, I understand what you're saying. You're saying a man can be dead in his flesh, but his spirit lives; but I respect my flesh too, and I know my spirit and what it's like. . . .

VG: So when you say you don't believe in death . . .

MARLEY (firmly): I don't believe in death, neither in flesh nor in spirit.

VG: But I don't understand, because one minute you're saying you don't believe in death, and the next minute you say you'll be shot, and . . .

MARLEY: Yes, but you have to AVOID IT! Some people don't figure life's such a great thing, they don't know how long they can preserve it. Preservation is the gift of God, the gift of God is life, the wages of sin is death. When a man does wickedness, he's gone out there and dead.

VG: Oh, I thought you meant death didn't exist at all.

MARLEY: Death does not exist for me. I truly know God. He gives me this (life) and my estimation is: if he gives me this, why should he take it back? Only the Devil says that everybody has to die.

When Marley arrived at the clinic near Lake Tegern in the Bavarian Alps, his brain tumour had affected his movement, and he could not walk. The cancer was strangling the life out of his lungs and stomach. A few weeks later, he was walking to get his treatments. A miracle might have seemed natural. After all, only the Devil says that everybody has to die.

Typically, Marley checked the positive side of his predicament. He told the Daily Mail's medical correspondent, "I have gone inside myself more. I have had time to explore my beliefs. And I

am the stronger because of it.'' Bob's locks were long gone. Chemotherapy does that. Whatever vanity Bob might have felt in his prime sensual health and physical beauty, its loss was confronted.

When Marley knew he was definitely dying, he started for home, Jamaica. He never quite made it, dying in a Florida hospital; but then so what, how often had Marley said Africa was his real home?

Besides, of the original fiery musical trinity, the Wailin' Wailers (Marley, Peter, Tosh and Bunny Livingston), those icebox-cool stepping razors, lethal rude boys, that pack of young lions that could quell a noisy crowd in Randy's Record Shop (hub of downtown Kingston's musical hot spots), with a single laser glance as they made their entrance; whose string of hits defined the new rude street mood month by month – Bob was meant to be the nomadic messenger. He was usually so cocooned by Rasta brothers and sisters wherever he went that he didn't need to absorb the local culture if he didn't want to. Over the years, the hordes of friends and fellow travellers seemed to multiply like locusts, covering the various plush carpets of the Wailers' comfortable service flats in London. Eventually, Marley had to resort to secretly booking extra rooms, and retreating from one suite to the next as the crowds became too oppressive.

But on some level, it must have suited him; Marley had a deep desire to 'bring the ghetto uptown' – that is, he needed the positive sides of ghetto living, aside from the poverty – the sense of community that people think of when they talk about 'roots'.

VG: Since you're always covering old tunes, I thought you should cover 'Rude Boy Get Bail', it's still so relevant. . . .

MARLEY: Well, Bunny did that in '66, when I was in America, but me did other rude boy songs – that rude boy business was bad, bad, music. Only them shouldn't have said rude boy, them shoulda said Rasta, you dig me? But in them times, me didn't know Rasta. Something was going on, you felt it, and didn't know if you were bad bad or good good – then I understood – it's good, you're good, it's Rasta!

VG: When or what made you realise it was Rasta, not rudeness?

MARLEY: What is there to benefit from badness? I wondered, I looked at it and thought, boy, bloodclaat, if I thump this man here, I feel the contact too. And then, I said, it's the same God that lives in my hand, and that means it's not him I thump, it's God I'm really thumping. So I used to wonder about this human feeling business . . . the whole thing is Rasta. The way I tell you, it's a whole experience, but you break it down and it's just – Rasta.

VG: Did you play lots of gigs in the early days?

MARLEY: Not a lot, just like Christmas and Easter morning, we'd be there up at the Carib Theatre (a Kingston venue, sweeping as a 1930's ocean liner stuck aground in the middle of a street market fringed with tiny record shacks, half-speakers. . . . Shows there are an institution like an old-time music hall, with all kinds of tiny tot dance troupes, magicians, mixing in with musicians). But (in a delighted voice) we was always the underground, always the rebels. We came from TRENCHTOWN. So you'd hear about Byron Lee (a popular middle of the road Jamaican bandleader, a kind of un-swinging Victor Sylvester), and all that society business, but we came from down so, named WAILERS, from TRENCHTOWN. So we stay, and we're glad of it. You've got to be someone.

VG: So now you get society knocking on your door . . .

MARLEY: Turn them off. Tell them to come another day.

(Interview conducted July '79.)

Bob's mother probably didn't like her son running wild in the streets. It is always good to have a trade – something you can fall back on, you'll always be in work. Bob, like many other reggae musicians, became a welder. Lots of sparks flying. Working alongside Bob was Desmond Dekker, the reggae singer who was to have one of Britain's first freak wildcat reggae hits when the original skins latched onto his braces-swingin' '007'. Alongside the bench, they would harmonise: Desmond wrote the songs. If you took a day off work, you lost your pay. So, if one day Desmond hadn't turned to laugh at someone's joke behind him, and a small piece of hot iron hadn't caught him in the eye – might things have been different?

It was Desmond who, on his days off while his eye was mending, started to push for recording time at Chinaman Leslie Kong's Beverleys label, and wound up with a big Jamaican hit, 'Honour Thy Father and Thy Mother'. Riding high on success, Desmond encouraged Bob to visit Beverleys with him. There, the generous-spirited reggae singer Jimmy Cliff (notable as Ivan, the hero of the film, The Harder They Come) set up an audition; Bob recorded a song. "It never really do nothing, but it was a good little song, named 'Judge Not'."

Bob was 15.

The Wailers came together in the simplest way. Bob was living in the house of the father of Bunny Livingston (now Wailer) in Trenchtown, the zinc shack shanty town ghetto side of Kingston – Kingston 12. Peter Tosh was a local youth who Bob and Bunny had seen around, singing and playing rhythm guitar. They rounded up a young singer called Junior Braithwaite, but he had to leave when his folks moved to the States; and the two women in the band, Rita Marley (Bob's future wife) and Beverley Kelso (whereabouts currently unknown) were phased out. Talking to Black Music's Carl Gayle in 1975, Bob said: "Them was good in recording but fe go pon stage and make a mistake that don't record over . . . (he laughs). But them sisters there, did great. They could sing high."

By now, the Wailers were leaders in the Kingston music scene, admired and emulated for their swaggering cool. Tosh was the tall, lean one with a rebel spirit like a bludgeon on songs like '400 Years'· Bunny was the spiritual one, with the high, sweet voice. Bob was the front man – the sensual singer-songwriter. Each of the trio had a well-defined presence. On even the earliest album sleeves, Bob can out-stare a lens in dread fashion, sending a sombre shiver down the years; presence that can't be bought. They were the spokesmen for the rude boys, the hustlers, scufflers and street survivors that walked with a stroll in their stride, scamming bank-roll schemes to make their dreams of movie star cars come true.

With Beverleys Records, the Wailers cut bouncy, spiritual pop, sometimes verging on gospel. Certain tunes – the cheerful sensuality of 'Do It Twice' (*Baby, you're so nice, I'd like to do the same thing twice*) and the Biblical admonitions of 'Caution' – suggest that the Wailers are more than a dance combo.

But the Wailers' rebel rude boy personality really gelled with their string of hits at Coxsone Dodd's Studio One label (backed by the Skatalites, the legendary sessioneers: Don Drummond, Roland Alphonso, Tommy McCook, Jackie Mittoo, Rico Rodriguez, Bobby Ellis, Jah Jerry, et al). The legendary producer, whose reputation for hit rhythms – not to mention seasonal revivals of old favourite tunes in different cover versions – hasn't slowed down in two decades, took such a shine to Bob that he let him use a room in the back of the studio to sleep in. Sadly, such generosity stopped short of the wallet: in 1966, the Wailers hit with 'Put It On', 'Rude Boy', 'I'm Still Waiting' and 'Rule Them Rudie', helping Dodd's bank account more than somewhat. "And so," Bob reminisced with Carl Gayle, Black Music's dread journalist, in 1975, "we expect to get some money, for this is Christmas.

Mrs. Cedella Booker, Bob Marley's mother.

Then the guy give me £60.00 after we make so much hits. So me just leggo and go live with me mother in America. Over there now, me find the music still in me. Singing and writing some good tunes like 'Bend Down Low'. . . ."

Bob joined the pool of immigrant casual labour, working in the Chrysler car plant, in a chemical factory. He remembered the time: "As a youth I was always active, never lazy. I learnt a trade, welding, so dealing with those things is part of my thing. I enjoy dealing with parts, part-work, and I never really mind because I just did it as much as I wanted to do it. Any time I felt fed up, I didn't really look for a job.

"I come from country, and country is always good. You grow everything. You don't really have to go out there and kill yourself to get a place or have money, you can eat and bathe and make clothes and build your own house . . . but in a strange land you can't find a place or settle down to find a way to organise. The best way out is to organise and leave. . . ." (Interview July '79.)

Marley's enthusiasm for the American way of life evaporated on receipt of a draft card, inviting him to partake in the Vietnam War. His views of direct action evolved over the years; interviewed by Neil Spencer in New Musical Express in 1975, the militant leader said: "Me don't want fight no guy with no guns. Me mustn't fight for my rights, my rights must come to me. You stand up for your right and don't give up the fight" (quoting from 'Get Up, Stand Up'), "but you don't fight for your right." Let alone fighting in Vietnam.

Home in Jamaica again, Marley found that although he was a known hit-maker, the rip-offs didn't fade away. They say the Beatles started out with a crummy contract, but their Jamaican equivalent was still hanging round trying to catch the producer's eye to get paid. Royalty cheques were alien as central heating in Jamaica.

Man to man is so unjust, children, you don't know who to trust. Your worst enemy could be your best friend, and your best friend your worst enemy. Some will eat and drink with you, then behind them sooss upon you. Only your friend know your secret, so only he could reveal it. Who the cap fit, let them wear it . . . ('Who The Cap Fit': **Rastaman Vibration**)

Hypocrites and parasites, they come up and take a bite. But eventually, Marley saw many of his dearest dreams come true – he played in Africa, for example, and he set up a viable artist-controlled record company and studio in Kingston, complete with record shop, and a distribution network for other artists' independent labels. It was even located in the old offices of Island Records – his ex-employers. The stranglehold that reggae musician after musician has complained of in the original shoal of producers (typified in the dictatorial, condescending, patronising record producer in The Harder They Come) was gradually being broken, as artists banded together, instead of working in competition.

But before the Tuff Gong label was any more than a sweet dream, Marley's first label, Wailing Soul (named after Rita's harmony trio, the Soul-ettes) was to collapse too, through bad organisation, and blatant bootlegging of hits like 'Bend Down Low' when it was number one in the Jamaican charts. Bunny Wailer's prison sentence on a ganja charge didn't help.

Who is Mr. Brown? I wanna know now. He is nowhere to be found . . . (he's) controlled by remote. Ohhhh – calling duppy conqueror. I'm the ghost catcher. . . . Take your chance – prove yourself! Oh yeah! Down in (the) Parade, people running like a masquerade. The police make a raid . . . What a thing in town! Crows, chauffeur-driven around! Skanking as if they had never known the man they call Mr. Brown. I can tell you where he's found. . . . ('Mr. Brown': **African Herbsman**)

It's usually said that when the Wailers joined Chris Blackwell's label, Island Records, access to unlimited studio time provided by

Early publicity photos.

Tuff Gong Studio at Marley's home, Hope Road.

Blackwell's passionate belief in the band kicked reggae forward like a football with the 1973 **Catch A Fire** album. But the most dramatic leap happened when Lee 'Scratch' Perry, the Upsetter, stopped working with Dodd, organising his regular talent shows, and began to produce the Wailers for his own Upsetter label in 1969. Released in England through Trojan Records (Bob always swore he never saw a penny from those Upsetter Trojan releases) **Rasta Revolution** and **African Herbsman** (plus the now deleted **Soul Rebels**) dumped acid in reggae's water supply. Early intimations of dub twirl Bob's voice in front of distorting mirrors with shuddering echo. Marley and Perry: a magnificent creative clash. The frisky, elfin producer has always seemed to hear differently from anybody else. Usually the awesome inventiveness of his production swamps the personality of the musicians he's producing, but with Marley's delivery refining and disciplining itself, and such good songs to work on, Scratch meets his match. Songs from **African Herbsman** like 'Kaya', 'Sun Is Shining' and 'Rock The Boat' are ice-cream yummy on the 1978 **Kaya** album; in the Scratch originals they sound surreal.

Working with Scratch, Marley, Peter and Bunny met the Barrett Brothers, Carly the drummer and Aston 'Family Man' the bassie. Fams had built his own bass, around 1967, out of a piece of board and four guitar strings. His obvious talent propelled him to more sophisticated instruments; when the Wailers began to record for Scratch, the relationship deepened till Fams and Carly threw in their session work as the Hippy Boys (session players for Sonia Pottinger's Tip Top label) and the Upsetters (for Scratch), to become the Wailers' rhythm section. The liaison worked for almost two decades.

The Wailers were already re-forming the set of social relations that had existed in Jamaican music. The producers dealt with individuals among the musicians, and the employees had no protection against any little skanks – tricks – they might pull. It was unusual for singers, or vocal trios and musicians to group together. In '75, Family Man's apple cheeks widened even more when he explained to Carl Gayle: "Five years we been like this, as one. Bob is the leader for the Wailers and I am the leader for the musical part of the group. The Wailers was the best vocal group, and I group was the best little backing band at the time. So we say, why don't we come together and smash the world."

Slave driver, the table is turned, catch a fire . . . you gonna get burned. Every time I hear the crack of the whip, my blood runs cold. I remember on the slave ship how they brutalised my very soul. . . .
('Slave Driver': **Catch A Fire**)

Marley's spirit interested Chris Blackwell as soon as they met. Marley's eyes were alert, awake to the action just out of vision. The face of a poet and fighter, an intensity that would burn from a page as much as in a song. Blackwell comes from a wealthy white colonial family, but he had a spirit of his own. When he began Island Records, it wasn't from a plush-carpeted West End office, but legging it round the black neighbourhoods of London – cycling round Dalston's record shacks in North London, selling records in the Portobello Road street market in Ladbroke Grove . . .

There's a much-loved story about Blackwell getting lost as a child, and finding himself in a Rasta encampment on the river. He discovered that the people who helped him, fed him, weren't the wild bogey-men he, along with most white Jamaican children, had been taught to avoid, even fear – the 'Blackheart Men'. A fairy-tale introduction for the white man most responsible for spreading the Rasta message, whether he believes in it or not. "What Bob stands for and what the Wailers are is so strong and so valid that I just feel that it is worth promoting as much as possible . . . I think that rock music has become a bit stale. . . ." he told Carl Gayle.

Blackwell made a simple act of faith and business sense. He financed the Wailers to record a stereo album with technical facilities unheard of for a Jamaican album. The mock Zippo lighter sleeve was so snazzy it must have been one of the first albums bought for the packaging alone. The marriage of reggae and Western marketing was astonishingly successful; the Zippo lighter nestled into innumerable student record collections along with Bowie and the Eagles. For reggae sound systems, a new Wailers release was already the bread, the butter and the jam, too.

The singing trinity of Bob, Peter and Bunny responded in different ways. It's often said that they split just before total confrontation with a Western audience simply because they all had their various works to do. Peter's almost bully-boy public swagger, and Bunny's serious spirituality were too intense to be contained in backing singing, perhaps; the Wailers, like most supremely popular groups, were loved individually as well. Media marketing's thirst for one single person to promote and identify and glorify was met half-way by Bunny's decision to stop touring. The weather outside Jamaica was as dread as the lack of ganja; Bunny retrenched after one tour of universities and a charismatic show at London's Speakeasy in 1973. It's not surprising that Peter, a super-assertive type who uses arrogance the way a builder uses a drill, split off to try and plough his own furrow alongside Bob's. He's got a mouth to match his remarkable height; this microphone wasn't big enough for the both of them.

Bunny settled himself in his farm in rural Bull Bay, surrounded by patches of exotic herbs flown in by far-flung admirers, it's said. Bunny's got a laser gaze that can alter the temperature in a room instantly. He descends from the hills to make records about his view of the politrickal (*it's a tug of war game, and the people are the rope*) and spiritual situation of the world, averaging a song every couple of months on his Solomonic label, while working towards his ambition: to be able to feed all of Jamaica on the produce from his farm. Meanwhile, Peter worked on his militant ganja man image, with the help of Family Man and Carly's spiritual successors as Prime Ministers of Reggae Rhythm, bassie Robbie Shakespeare and drummie Sly Dunbar. He attempted to bring the rock market to its knees by a liaison with those unabashed jet-set decadents, the Rolling Stones. Peter's noisy demands for equal rights and justice didn't ignite on contact with the former Satanic Majesties (self-titled) and Peter's music began to sound flatter and more hectoring, like the interminable drone of a nagging, frustrated school teacher confronted with disobedient, unreasonable, non-record-buying kids. This particular flirtation with Babylon didn't reap the anticipated rewards.

The international rock charts always beam and beckon, tease and tantalise Jamaican musicians. Happy go lucky, middle of the road attempts to bland out rhythms and lyrics for the Zion of radio airplay often point the arrow downhill for a reggae singer attempting to follow up a one-off chart hit, to 'do a Marley', and stay on top. It's rather like spending all your money on a pot of caviar to gratify your beloved, then finding out they're allergic to fish – and you'd have rather had eggs, anyway.

Blackwell's ambition to break Bob into the rock market was fuelled by more than everyday commercialism. His respect for Bob was matched by a personal affection – and his instinct wasn't misplaced. Bob bridged the gap between black and white by more than blood. His close-cropped, jump-cut lyrics are taut as a haiku, baring level after level as you listen; his passionate songs of Rasta, of international and local politics, were always pitched from a peoples-eye perspective, unlike the monolithic sloganeering of so many would-be revolutionist singers. The process of Marley being accepted, though never colonised, by the rock audience begins with the eloquent rock guitar leads on **Catch A Fire** (overdubbed by American session man Wayne Perkins), that didn't derange the ears of a generation weaned on the Cream and Neil Young. The Wailers' 'crossover appeal' to rock ear was generally based on the guitar work, and smooth production.

As Marley re-formed the Wailers after Peter and Bunny left in 1974 (his early mentor Joe Higgs, the folk-flavoured protest singer, stood in for Bunny for a while) he recruited a new crew of musicians, spanning poles of international black cults – guitsie Al Anderson, more used to the New York art scene than Dread, Junior Marvin, a flashy guitarist with heavy metal tendencies from Ladbroke Grove, and Tyrone Downie, who'd been hanging round the Wailers scene from when he was an inquisitive little youth. Tyrone in particular is all boisterous nervous energy and crazy-or-not-so-crazy careening ideas. The three of them took a while to find their level in this new-look Wailers that fused so many elements of black experience. Backing singers were the I Threes – Bob's wife the remarkable Rita Marley (though Marley had denied the marriage in early interviews, their deep understanding remained constant), Judy Mowatt and Marcia Griffiths. All three were popular singers in their own right, strong personalities whose capabilities always outshone the allocated echo/repeat function of backup singing. Judy kept her own Ashandan record label going, releasing the **Black Woman** album, which is the strongest Rasta woman's statement yet. Marcia, an African princess with a stately dowager air, and partly responsible (along with the sadly underrated Bob Andy), for half of Bob and Marcia's early hit, 'Young, Gifted and Black', has a successful solo crooner career, and Rita Marley is beginning to step forward again with her **Who Feels It Knows It** album.

Elements of this high-powered team created the album that stamped Marley's name indelibly on rock consciousnesses, and set the seal on the psyche of a generation of black youth, **Natty Dread**.
I! Rebel music! I! Rebel music!
Take my soul and suss me out
Check my life if I'm in doubt
3 o'clock – roadblock
And hey, Mr. Cop ain't got no
(What you say down there)
Ain't got no birth certificate on me now . . .
('Rebel Music (3 O'clock Roadblock)': **Natty Dread**)

For many black youths, Marley came just in time. There had been no inspirational movement to identify with since the Black

The I-Threes.

Panthers, and many youths were alarmed by some 'freedom fighters' ideas of flinging a home-made Molotov through the window of the pub down the road. **Natty Dread** presented a forceful, positive image of Rasta, burning with righteous anger and determination. It was serious music, reality music, dealing with their own everyday degradations and petty brutalisations that Marley was also experiencing as an 'anti-social' dread in Jamaica, played in a roots reggae pounding style, but flavoured with other cultures – not quite a mixed marriage of a music, but a definite flirtation.

Rasta gave black youth a new, dread way of walking, with head high and proud, and an incentive to check their roots. For some people, that meant changing their accent to sound more like visiting Jamaicans. For others, it meant learning Amharic. Changing your name to lose the colonial slave label and re-claim a new, African identity.

The idea of a place where you belong is seductive, if where you are conspires constantly to make you feel unwanted, by harassment and rejection on every level.

A dreadlock congo bongo I
Children get your culture.
('Natty Dread')

Marley was out there, indomitable, beautiful, speaking the truth and actually making money at it! Even the fact that a black man could retain his dignity and integrity and still be an internationally respected star, was an inspiration. From the **Burnin** album with its grinding 'Rastaman Chant', and peaking in a frenzy at **Natty Dread** time, black youth in Britain as well as Jamaica started to break their combs and brave the flak from the family.

The time was right, and the weave of the music was so tight. On **Natty Dread**, Marley's songs present a complete package, invoking revolution and Revelation, sex and poverty, pain, anger and compassion. He homes in on textural details that haul the audience right into the action:

Said I remember when we used to sit
In the government yard in Trenchtown
Observing the hypocrites
Mingle with the good people we meet . . .
And then Georgie would make the fire lights,
I seh, log would burnin' thru the nights
Then we would cook cornmeal porridge,
. . . Of which I'd share with you
My feet is my only carriage
So I've got to push on through. . . .
('No Woman No Cry': **Natty Dread**)

Marley's entry into England was accompanied by a blaze of promotion; he grabbed all the music paper front covers, despite the subcutaneous racism of most mass media. The Lyceum show recorded on the **Live!** album was a fever-pitch affair, with the red and gold baroque music-hall interior of the Lyceum seeming to shrink to a small club, so complete was the power of the Wailers' control, penetrating into the furthest ornate wedding-cake opera box. The intensity of that one show propelled Marley's career instantly; Rasta was suddenly the over-riding lifestyle and image for all the militant black youth in their khaki fatigues, and the rebel outlaw stance mesmerised rock kids who hadn't had a hit of uncut energy from a musician since the Stones went soft, in the early 70's.

'Cos I feel like bombing a church,
Now I know that the preacher is lying . . .
('Talking Blues': **Natty Dread**)

"Politics and church are the same thing," Marley said to Neil Spencer of the New Musical Express, shortly before the Lyceum show. "Politicians are devils, devils who corrupt. They don't smoke 'erb (ganja) because when you smoke you think alike, and they don't want that."

Marley's super-militant stance disavowed conventional organised politics as much as the established churches. He had scant regard for the school of thought that Rasta was merely an extension of engrained colonial thinking, based on a Bible translated by white supremacists to corset the minds of subjugated races – an attitude found in many revolutionary political circles.

MARLEY: What one man thinks is great. But only a fool leans upon his one understanding. The truth is there. King Solomon and King David are the roots of black people and the roots of creation – they are Jacob's people. So when a black man says that Rasta is colonialist, he's turning it the other way in the sense of diplomacy, he's putting down his own thing, because he's learnt how to do it. Who teaches him? You dig what I'm saying?

VG: Many British blacks think it's more important to confront the reality in England than to think about repatriating to Africa.

MARLEY: I could agree with that, but why fight to stay in a place that's dirty, where the rivers are polluted? Why stay in a place where if God shook two earthquakes, all these stones are gonna fall on you and kill you? Africa for Africans, at home and abroad . . . we're not saying that people can't mix together. But this world is funny, because you claim you're white and I claim I'm black, and we have a fight because if you're not sensible, it becomes a barrier. (Here he alludes to Biblical lines of descent.) But the truth is the truth, your father's name is Noah and my father's name is Noah, and Shem's father named Noah, so we all three people came from Noah. So we all three people come from Noah, so we're the same people. . . .

VG: But where do you struggle? Do you feel a Rasta musician shouldn't become politically involved?

MARLEY: I don't involve myself. We don't support either the JLP or the PNP . . . we know that we are Rastafarians, that we have something to offer. We have the Twelve Tribes of Israel, the Ethiopian Orthodox Church, the Theocratic Government. If a youth wants to go out there and fight politics, he can go. We have something that demands rights if you stand where me stand. If you don't do that, you'll be dying in the street with your dreadlocks on, because you're not defending the thing you must defend. You can't be strong, you must be a weakling. We defend His Majesty (Emperor Haile Selassie of Ethiopia, the living God of Rasta) philosophy. It's not political – it's only words that make it political. It's life – people – action. . . .

(Interview July '79.)

The old Island House, Hope Road, was full of iry (pleasant, enjoyable) feelings in 1976. Marley had enjoyed the European tour, having fun winding up all the journalists who displayed blank incomprehension of his beliefs – or even hostility – by sinking into a deeper and deeper Jamaican patois. 'Roots Rock Reggae', one of his slightest songs, from the American-flavoured **Rastaman Vibrations**, had entered the American Top Ten. He returned to Jamaica, to the open extended family way of living at the big old colonial mansion, now a haven for Jamaican society's rejects, the Dreads; constantly discriminated against in jobs, in housing, in so many ways; Hope Road was more than an uptown hang-out, it was a fort in enemy territory.

Feeling up, feeling down, this feeling wouldn't leave me alone; then I came on one that said – "Hey dread! Smile, natty dread!" Get it together in Jamaica. Soulful town, soulful people, I see you're having fun, dancing to the reggae rhythm – oh island in the sun! Come on and smile, you're in Jamaica! . . . ('Smile Jamaica')

When Marley talked about natural mystics, he was drawing from life. Despite the upfull feelings of the time, promoted by the Wailers in their 1976 'Smile Jamaica' single, the temperature was rising for the coming Jamaican elections. Marley had agreed to play a concert supporting the Peoples National Party of Michael Manley – with Cuban, as opposed to American, links – the opposition being the Jamaican Labour Party. Socialist Manley

had agreed to legalise herb (always a popular political stance for politicians trying to catch votes, that somehow never seems to materialise). One night, sleeping in the bright, airy bedroom at Hope Road, with its colourful hangings and cushions, Bob flinched, dreaming of gunfire. The premonition coloured his thoughts. Typically, he translated the warnings into melody. At night, when the Piccadilly Circus hubbub of the day had died down, he would sit in a tiny shoebox of a bedroom, playing his acoustic guitar, toying with fragments of songs swimming from his subconscious.

One particular night, it was a song that would appear on the **Exodus** album the next year. The room was jammed with the youths that had played table tennis all day on the veranda outside, hushed women drawing their skirts over their knees as they squatted in a corner, listening intently to Bob as he sang: *These are the big fish that always eat down the small fish . . . they would do anything to materialise their every wish. . . .* pushing and pulling on the words till the room almost crackled with static. One young woman sat on the far edge of the bed, gazing intently at Bob as if he was a snake-charmer. Marley's frown cleared for a moment the deep groove that was soon to be permanently etched between his brows. Smiling at the delighted woman, he changed gear; without stopping, he shifted the shape of the song to a less sorrowful, more sinuous rock on the guitar, a light-hearted seducer about making the bed-springs squeak. The overlap of emotions was all a part of the iry feelings, all part of life – people – action; of Rasta, Bob would probably have said. The tearing, anguished omens of his song about callousness, selfishness and greed drifted away. Two weeks later, Bob's dreams of guns materialised not 200 yards away.

Ambush in the night – four guns aiming at me . . . they open fire on me . . . see them fighting for power, but they know not the hour. So they bribe us, with their guns and spare parts and money, trying to belittle our integrity. . . . ('Ambush In The Night': **Survival**)

"Every song we sing come true, you know. It all happens in real life. Some songs are too early, some happen immediately, but all of them happen. Burning and looting happen – so much time, it's a shame. The curfew. Yeeees, mon – everything happen. . . . I don't have to sing no more song, just that one line – just, 'guiltiness rest on their conscience'. . . ." (Interview conducted May '77.)

When the gun-fire started outside the rehearsal room, the afternoon before the Manley show, most of the Wailers thought it was Carly the drummer tapping out some new militant rhythm on his hi-hat. Then the door opened, and the muzzle of the gun appeared.

For a split second, everyone was transfixed: the instant of watching the wasp, the question of waking before it stings. Then, as Marley recalled in a later interview (Neil Spencer: New Musical Express '75): "I can't *tell* you. I wasn't even *there*. There was a struggle, and then me didn't know wha'appen. . . . But I'll tell you, during the time it happen, a real *mystic* a come in. Funny . . . Jah guide I and protect." Marley was saved by the Wailers' manager, Don Taylor, who flung himself in front of Bob. For a while, it seemed as if Taylor, rushed to hospital in Miami, wouldn't be able to walk. He recovered. So did Rita Marley, injured outside by gunfire even before the Wailers had time to realise what was going on and dash for safety in the bathroom – the only accessible place with a door.

The five gunmen have never been officially identified. It seems reasonable to suppose that they were emissaries of the hotter-than-hot political tribal wars of Kingston, where each area is controlled – bought in exchange for favours like homes and food – by political parties. Political allegiances in Kingston can easily be a life or death matter, like religion in Northern Ireland. Some local rumours pinned the blame on a racetrack involvement of Marley's. Marley prided himself on being a ghetto survivor, and he wasn't far from appreciating a nicely turned piece of badness by an entertaining Johnny Too Bad. Some of his friends, it's said, would take advantage of his generosity; there was one incident where Bob, sitting watching TV at his home, was staggered to see the licence number of his BMW (an obvious auto choice – not just that they're nippy, the initials stand for Bob Marley and the Wailers), come up on the police wanted listings. An enterprising friend had casually borrowed Marley's car, without telling him it was needed for a bank robbery. In 1981, Winston, the brother of Bob's friend Claudie Massop (himself shot in cold blood by the police), was killed in a quarrel with a jockey at a race track. In the ghetto, survival is a must, and Bob hadn't cocooned himself away from ghetto reality in any ivory tower.

You're running and you're running and you're running away – but you can't run away from yourself. . . . You must have done something wrong . . . something you don't want nobody to know about, you must have . . . no, no, no, I'm not running away, I've got to protect my life, and I don't want to live with no strife. It is better to live on the house top than to live in a house full of confusion, so I made my decision and I left you. . . . ('Running Away': **Kaya**)
He who fights and runs away, lives to fight another day.
('Heathen': **Exodus**)

Marley played the scheduled concert, then beat a tactical retreat to neighbouring Miami, where a whole host of brethren and sistren (sisters) ensured he wasn't in any more isolation than he wanted.

He only returned to Jamaica at the request of his brother Claudie Massop, an energetic Kingston entrepreneur, highly respected in former reggae producer Edward Seaga's Jamaica Labour Party. Claudie had joined forces with Bucky Marshall, a ferret-like captain in the opposing politrickal army. Manley's Peoples National Party. Legend has it that when they found themselves in the same prison cell, the two decided to banish the petty but lethal squabbles that were killing off the ghetto youth to the benefit of politicians alone. Both men are dead now, so we cannot know exactly how they decided to set up a Peace Treaty, and mark the occasion with a major concert. Marley's triumphant homecoming was to set the seal on the new spirit of hopeful resolution.

The concert, held in the concrete bowl of the National Arena, was a great media success, and a musical delight. Marley seemed overjoyed to be back in Jamaica. Bunny Wailer refused to appear at the One Love Peace Concert – perhaps the wise man anticipated the forlorn pricked balloon of good intentions the Peace Treaty would soon become.

Culture, Trinity, Althia and Donna, Dennis Brown, Big Youth, the lusty Jacob Miller bemoaning on stage his 'divorce' from his girlfriend, waggling his tumultuous hips, and trying to haul policemen onto the stage to smoke spliffs with him . . . Peter Tosh rounding on politicians of both parties from the stage, defiantly hauling on a spliff while Sly Dunbar and Robbie Shakespeare (racing across the stage wielding his bass like a bayonet), rolled and thundered behind him . . . it was an eventful show. But as soon as Marley appeared, the full moon shining directly over his head, the show was *his* by popular consent. Fulfilling the audience's shamanistic demands on him, he called the rival leaders, Seaga and Manley, onto the stage, and made them clasp hands in a triumphal arch over his dread, that symbol of antisocial behaviour in the worlds of the leaders – who were obeying his demands, for once.

The next morning Marley smoked a peaceful spliff on the verandah. He talked of people anticipating violence on that full moon. "They said it would be red, but it was – *red-eye* (stoned)!" he laughed. With so much goodwill around, it still seems odd that it took so long for the Jamaican police to discover who among their ranks was responsible for the shooting of Peace Treaty organiser Claudie Massop a few weeks later.

There's a natural mystic blowing in the air; if you listen carefully now, you will hear. This could be the first trumpet – might as well be the last. Many more will have to suffer, many more will have to die. Don't ask me why. Things are not the way they used to be, I won't tell no lie. One and all have to face reality, now. . . . ('Natural Mystic': **Exodus**)

Before Bob returned to play the Peace Concert, he had spent some time in London working on **Exodus**. Those sessions were exhilarating, from the breathless games of table football with Aswad, the London reggae group of young Dreads that Bob could plainly check as his spiritual children, back to the studio. When producer Chris Blackwell liked the sound he and engineer Karl Pitterson were getting, he'd ask one of the large group that always gathered at the mixes to call 'the Skip' – Bob being the Skipper. On the night that the triumphant march of **Exodus** was mixed, the control room was almost shaking with steppers' (dancers') enthusiasm, Marley himself leaning against the back wall with eyes shut, arms crossed, till he suddenly clicked tightly with the rhythm and hurled himself into transfigured dancing motion, gymnast free and athletic. All the stage presence that normally filled stadiums scintillated around the studio. The triumphant rhythm seemed to tie a ribbon of invincibility round that mood, that moment.

Times were interesting in London. Punk was in full bloom, and groups like Aswad played for Rock Against Racism with the Clash. The tune of the year was Culture's classic, 'Two Sevens Clash'; it was generally felt that 1977 was somehow a significant year. On 7.7.77, many Jamaicans actually stayed home for fear of a Biblical holocaust; but nothing unusually dread happened that day. Since Don Letts, the dread DJ at the Roxy Club, had turned the inner core of punks on to reggae, and Johnny Rotten had played a dazzling selection of reggae on the radio, a whole generation of white youth was as obsessed as their black school-mates with the works of the Joe Gibbs and Channel One studios. Reggae was the crucial to-be-colonised black music for punks, as r'n'b had been to the 60's white rock generation.

The Wailers were the most international reggae combo, and their musical progression moved in isolation from Jamaican reggae development; their smooth latter-day productions never plunged headlong into full-blooded dub (that great Jamaican music speciality of re-juggled, re-energised rhythm tracks – dismantling and rebuilding them in the studio with delay, echo and reverb) for example, though Family Man's sensibility always lay close to the heart of dub, and their old associate Scratch was a remarkable pioneer of the genre.

Right on time, Lee Perry arrived to stay in a flat in Island's Basing Street Studios, where the Wailers were mixing **Exodus**. Bob spent a lot of time there, reasoning with his old spar (companion) who he openly referred to as 'a genius!' There, the two of them first heard punk band the Clash's version of Scratch's haunting production of 'Police and Thieves' by singer Junior Murvin. Punks seemed as weirdly alien to Marley as he himself had seemed to earlier rock fans. He teased a woman who'd punk-bleached her hair – "You should have dyed it red, green and gold (the Rasta Ethiopian colours)!" But listening to the bizarre, unexpected amphetamine punk version of Murvin's pleading song (dealing with overlapping criminal and police activities), Bob became intrigued by the connections: punks with their extravagantly coloured and cropped hair, Rastas with their locks, both openly expressing their commitment to a life outside the conventional majority of society, both harassed and persecuted by the authorities just like the Kingston rudies were in the 60's . . . even the unglamorous anti-chic that punk made chic fitted in with the way Bob liked to wear denims and tracksuits on stage as well as off, so that the youth in the audience wouldn't admire his outfit, feel frustrated, and be forced to hustle for style. "In a way,"

Marley mused, "me like see them safety-pins and t'ing. Me no like do it myself, y'understand, but me like see a man can suffer pain without crying."

In spontaneous spirit, Marley and Scratch went into the studio with members of Aswad (though some Wailers later added music) and cut a song called 'Punky Reggae Party' – not a great song, but once again, Marley had encapsulated the moment: *Rejected by society, treated with impunity* . . . Bob sang of the two tribes, punks and Dreads.

While **Exodus** was vastly out-sold by Culture's contemporary heavy roots in punk shops like Rough Trade, it proved to be a commercial goldmine for the Wailers. Track after track smashed up the charts – 'Exodus', 'Jamming', 'Waiting In Vain', 'Three Little Birds' – it was clear Marley hadn't been waiting in vain.

When the morning gathers the rainbow – want you to know, I'm a rainbow too. So to the rescue – here I am! Want you to know just, if you can, where I stand! ('Sun Is Shining': **Kaya**)

When **Kaya** was released, it was greeted coldly by most critics – though Bob, author of the line, *I do not expect to be justified by the laws of man*, very likely swore, then laughed when he read the accusations that he'd become a 'weakheart'. **Kaya** is an exquisite confection, candy-floss that doesn't make you sick. His love songs are witty (*She made it thru the exit, she just couldn't take it* – 'She's Gone') and disarmingly modest (*We'll share the shelter of my single bed* – 'Is This Love'). Long-time Wailers fans resented the fact that three of the tracks at least – 'Sun Is Shining', 'Kaya' and 'Satisfy My Soul' – were already well known from the old Scratch-produced albums. Old-timers missed that head-spinning 3-D Scratch treatment.

"These people!" Bob snorted in derision to Black Music's Chris May. "My inspiration come from the Most High. Me a free being pon this earth and me do what me want to do. The world don't control me. Them songs great, and me love them, that's why I do them over. And me might do them over *again* pon the next album if me feel them nice still!"

Later, Marley re-assessed **Kaya** in relation to the shooting at Hope Road; it was generally felt that maybe Marley had taken a less militant stance than usual to avert more aggro. "People don't understand that we live in this earth too," said Bob seriously, passionately. "We don't sing these songs and live in the sky. I don't have an army behind me – if I did, I wouldn't care, I'd just get *more militant*! Because I'd know, well, I have 50,000 armed youth and when I talk, I talk from strength. But you have to know how you're dealing. Maybe if I'd tried to make a heavier tune than **Kaya** they would have tried to assassinate me because I would have come too hard. I have to know how to run my life, because that's what I have, and nobody can tell me to put it on the line, you dig? Because no-one understands these things. These things are heavier than anyone can understand. People that aren't involved don't *know* it, it's *my* work, and I know it outside in. I know when I am in danger and what to do to get out. I know when everything is cool, and I know when I tremble, do you understand?"

Marley was speaking at the time of the 1979 Reggae Sunsplash Festival in Montego Bay, Jamaica's tourist ghetto; it was the Wailers' first Jamaican show since the Peace Concert. Once again, audience ecstasy proved Marley still held the heart of the Jamaican people. The familiar gestures – the Christ-like stretching out of the arms, the neo-Nijinsky skipping on the spot while his dreadlocks flailed the air – that seemed clichéd on an off night in the middle of a gruelling international tour (and had become the dominant mode – or cliché – of too many other reggae musicians), were refurbished. When Marley announced a new song and played 'Ambush In The Night' with its reference to Jah Rastafari saving him from the attack at Hope Road, the audience tuned in to his words with an immediacy that showed his predicament had been deeply felt.

Meanwhile, Marley was mixing the **Survival** album in his own Tuff Gong studio that embodied so many of his daydreamings over the years. Excellent facilities in low-tech Jamaica, no more travelling to London or Miami to mix tunes, plus: "Look into my yard. This is a ghetto you're looking at – I've just brought the ghetto uptown. My thing is, why must I stay in one place every day of my life, and all the days of my life I have to run from the police? Look in any other yard along the road (Hope Road being a gracious uptown boulevard, with the Prime Minister's mansion next door to Marley's yard) and see if you see any one of my brethren out there in any other yard. When I lived in the ghetto, every day I had to jump fences, police trying to hold me, you dig? So my job all the while was to try to find one place where the police wouldn't run me down too much.

"So I don't want to stay in contact with the ghetto, in contact with the ghetto means in contact with a prison . . . not the people. When the law comes out, they send them into the ghetto first, not uptown. So how long does it take you to realise – bwaoy, well, they don't send them uptown, y'know! So we'll make a ghetto uptown. EVERY DAY I jumped fences from the police, for YEARS, not a week. For YEARS. . . . You either stay there and let bad people shoot you down, or you make a move and show people some improvement. Or else I would take up a gun and start shoot them off, and then a lot of youths would follow me, and they'd be dead the same way. I want some improvement. It doesn't have to be materially, but it can be freedom of thinking."

Once his basic needs of food, shelter, transport and ganja were there, Bob never checked for money too much; quietly, without publicity, he'd been giving to build schools, hospitals – just giving it away where he felt it should go. Some said he had a hand in supplying guns to Africa – difficult to prove, but it would be in line with his uncompromising stand, which clarified further after he first played in Africa.

Check my soul if I'm in doubt, he sang years before. Now, with the militant phrases of 'Zimbabwe' thundering from the studio, Bob said: "I expect if you're living by the gun, if gun is the fight, then FIRE gun. If where you come from, you fight with sticks and stones, then fight with sticks and stones. If the fight is spiritual, then fight spiritual, because everywhere the fight goes on. We don't have any alternatives. . . . A lot of people defend South Africa, some secretly, some openly. A lot of white people defend South Africa, and when you keep the black man down in South Africa you keep him down all over the earth. Because Africa is Solomon's goldmine. So – war! Either I and I lives, or no-one lives. You know what the big fight is? It's that black people – and only black people – mustn't say the truth about Rasta . . . just imagine being a Rasta in this world which doesn't like Rasta. We could be enjoying being something else, but no."

Soon we'll find out who is the real revolutionary. ('Zimbabwe': **Survival**)

Marley being a Rasta rebel ensures that *We refuse to be what you wanted us to be – we are what we are, and that's the way it's going to be. Talking 'bout my freedom . . .* ('Babylon System': **Survival**). In other words, his views didn't conform to what many contemporary 'radical' people endorse; whether he was more radical than his critics, or less, is a matter of debate. Certainly, Black Music's Chris May appeared surprised when Marley told him he approved of the National Front because it would unite black people in opposition; rebel-spirited feminists might easily shudder at the old-fashioned pleasure Marley derived from seeing women switch to a nice skirt from their jeans and cover their hair. Not that he'd ever force the issue. *Can't tell the woman from the man, they are dressed in the same pollution,* as he mourned back in the old **Catch A Fire** days.

But Marley wouldn't care. With time, he grew more outspoken, if that were possible, openly scathing about the 'white man's shitstems' – "Let them perish in their own fucking SALT!" he shouted once, punning on the Strategic Arms Limitation Treaty, and the condiment which Rastas don't use. During the following year, Marley and the Wailers were on a non-stop international tour, acting as the messengers of Rasta. He was unconcerned about bending his music specifically to gratify foreign ears. "To tell you the truth, I don't even think that way," he said when asked about pressures to please the American market. "I just think more of an inner creativeness. Inna my chest," tapping his jumper as he spoke. "Me no really a prostitute, me just respect people like Taj Mahal and Bob Dylan – they respect their own talent, that means where they are and who they are. It's *that* that people have to want, you dig? 'Cos the people don't want to be pleased, they want to please someone, you dig – it goes both ways."

But someone will have to pay for the innocent blood that they shed every day. . . . We no know how we and them a go work this out. . . . But in the beginning Jah created everything, he gave man dominion over all things, but now it's too late, you see, men have lost their faith, eating up all the flesh from off the earth. . . . But we have no friends in a high society. . . . ('We And Them': **Uprising**)

Uprising was second only to **Exodus** in terms of sales, even though its message was a warrior charge, as specific in its rebellion and apocalyptic vision as the original Wailers ever were. Marley is unique in being the only international recording star who's stuck so close to his original rebel roots while the sales figures mount up. Marley had finally visited Ethiopia, after arduous years trying to get an entry visa. He told the Face's Roz Reines in New York, shortly before his collapse: "I defend Haile Selassie, but right now in Ethiopia, they don't like any talk of Selassie. The government there don't like Rasta either because them bring off propaganda and want to change to a kind of Russian tradition. So I man say it's nice to go there but I don't really feel that the strength is there. Not until things change with the government, and the people become the people again."

Other realisations that could have been disillusion were also reflected in **Uprising** – the chunky tune 'Bad Card' referred to the breakdown of relations between the Wailers and their authoritative long-term manager, Don Taylor. "Don too tricky, you know?" Marley told Reines. "They don't want fe trick you, them want fe trick your mind, that is the thing I don't like . . . you have eyes, you have ears, you can talk, you can smell, and yet him want fe trick your mind. Is better somebody ask you for something and get it rather than try to trick me fe take it. You can't trick me, I know who God is, so how can you trick me? I'm no fool."

He'd also played at the Independence Day celebrations in Zimbabwe (April 17th, 1980), where the crowds got so excited, the guards started spraying tear gas in the middle of 'I Shot The

Brighton 1980.

Sheriff". A return to the Promised Land, just as the Bible predicted for the wandering Jews. . . .

The Pope was shot in the same week that Marley died, and Dreads everywhere marvelled at the coincidence – Rastas believe the Pope is in cahoots with the Devil, and that the Vatican is the heart of Babylon's system. But then Marley died – albeit of natural causes – at a time when violent deaths of public figures were helter-skeltering upwards, a cycle that seemed to start with the assassination of John Lennon in New York at the end of 1980.

For years, Marley had been talking about just such a turmoil, as prophesied in the Book of Revelations. Where others – weakhearts, perhaps? – tremble at these repeated defamations of what had seemed the natural order, Marley wasn't phased. He'd read it all before, in the Bible. "It's the last days without a doubt. It's the last quarter before the year 2000, and righteousness – the positive way of thinking – must win. Good over evil. We're confident of victory."

That same quiet determination floods 'Redemption Song', the last track on Marley's last album, **Uprising**. (Last, theoretically, anyway; Wailers tracks will probably start tumbling from various producers' cupboards, where they'd slipped behind a shelf till the right time. . . .)

The last song on a last album; the only record of Bob playing his acoustic guitar, solo. An invitation to join in Marley's most intimate music. The message of this song seems very specific – it's a quiet song, but it shouts:

Old pirates, yes they rob I
Sold I to the merchants ships
Minutes after they took I from the bottomless pit
But my hand was made strong
By the hand of the Almighty
We forward in this generation triumphantly
All I ever had is songs of freedom
Won't you help to sing these songs of freedom
Cause all I ever had was redemption song.
Emancipate yourselves from mental slavery
None but ourselves can free our minds
Have no fear for atomic energy
Cause none of them can stop the time
How long shall they kill our prophets while we stand aside and look?
Some say it's just a part of it, we've got to fulfill the book. . . .

Catch A Fire

Bob in 1974.

(Above) Peter Tosh.
Bunny Livingstone Wailer (Left).

(Above) The surviving Wailers, 1974 (L. to R.: Aston (Family Man) Barrett, Bob Marley, Carlton (Carly) Barrett).

"Get up, stand up" – The Lyceum, London, July 1975.

The Lyceum, July 1975.

Aston (Family Man) Barrett.

Carlton (Carly) Barrett.

Al Anderson.

Alvin (Seeko) Patterson.

Tyrone Downie and son.

Al Anderson and Junior Marvin.

The I-Threes (Judy Mowatt, Rita Marley and Marcia Griffiths).

The Wailers. (Top row, L. to R.: Alvin (Seeko) Patterson, Earl (Wire) Lindo, Junior Marvin, Tyrone Downie; Bottom row, L. to R.: Aston (Family Man) Barrett, Al Anderson, Bob Marley, Carlton (Carly) Barrett).

Rita Marley.

Marley and some of the family at home, Hope Road.

Bunny Livingstone Wailer and Peter Tosh.

Lee (Scratch) Perry and son.

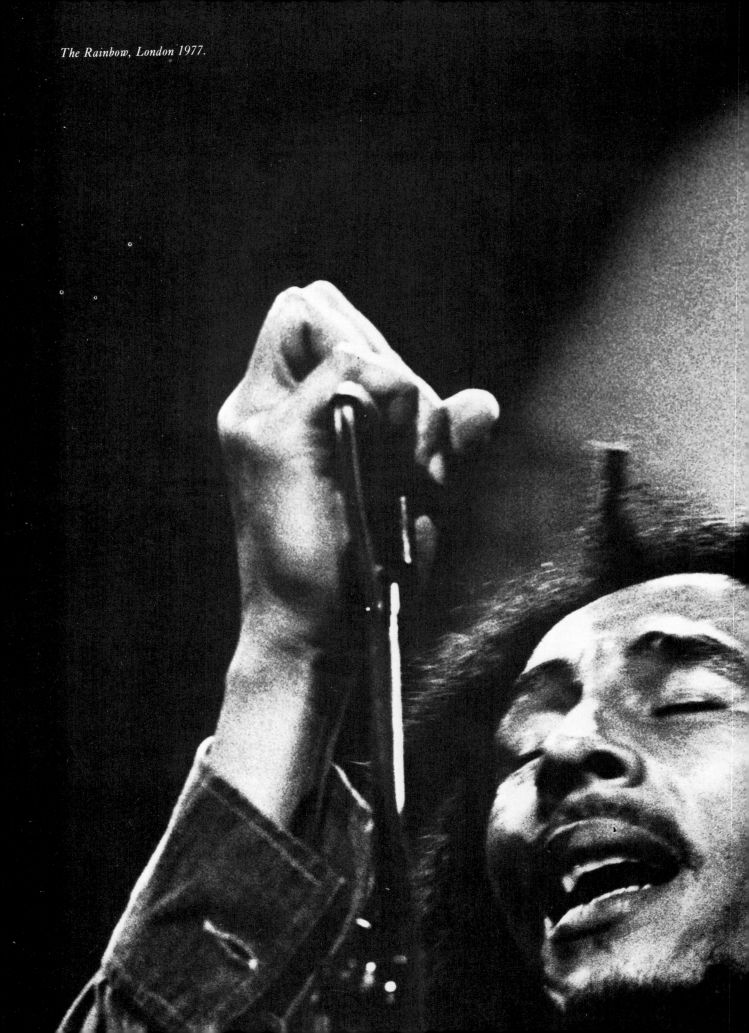

The Rainbow, London 1977.

Survival

Michael Manley, leader of the Peoples National Party.

Edward Seaga, leader of the Jamaica Labour Party, and Prime Minister at the time of Marley's death.

Marley with ghetto leader Claudie Massop before the Peace Concert.
Claudie was later shot dead by police.

Armed police at Hope Road, the morning of the Peace Concert.

The Peace Concert, April 1978.

*The climax of the Peace Concert, clasping hands
with Prime Minister Michael Manley
and opposition leader Edward Seaga.*

With Jacob Miller, singer with Inner Circle, who died in a car crash a year later.

Recording the **'Survival'** *album at Tuff Gong, July 1979.*

With Jacob Miller and Junior Marvin.

*"Africa unite
Cause we're moving right out of Babylon
And we're going to our father's land . . ."*

BOB MARLEY & THE WAILERS
ZIMBABWE

Babylon By Bus

Junior Marvin, Jacob Miller and Burning Spear – Reggae Sunsplash, July 1979.

Marley, Pam Nestor and Ijahman Levi at Reggae Sunsplash.

At a children's party, Keskidee Centre, London.

Playing football in Battersea Park, London.

L. to R.: A nameless Dread, Neville Garrick (Wailers art man),
Bob, Tony 'Gilly' Gilbert (Wailers Ital cook), Trevor Bow and
Derek from the Sons Of Jah.

At Crystal Palace Garden Party, June 1980.

The I-Threes at Crystal Palace.

At Essex House, New York, September 1980.

Backstage with The Commodores at Madison Square Gardens,
September 1980.

Leaving Essex House for the last concert.

The last concert.

Filming for the Agency of Public Information.

HON. ROBERT NESTA MARLEY O.M.

OFFICIAL FUNERAL SERVICE

FOR THE

HON. ROBERT NESTA MARLEY O.M.

(BOB MARLEY - BERHANE SELASSIE)

(Light of the Trinity)

AT

THE ETHIOPIAN ORTHODOX CHURCH
HOLY TRINITY

89 MAXFIELD AVENUE, KINGSTON, JAMAICA

8. 00 — 9. 00 a.m.

AND

THE NATIONAL ARENA

11. 00 a.m.

THURSDAY MAY 21, 1981.

OFFICIATING:-

HIS EMINENCE ABOUNA YESEHAQ
ARCHBISHOP OF THE ETHIOPIAN ORTHODOX CHURCH
IN THE WESTERN HEMISPHERE

Assisted by Priests and Deacons of the Ethiopian Orthodox Church in Jamaica.

SERVICE WILL BE PERFORMED IN GEEZ, AMHARIC AND ENGLISH

The day before the funeral the body of Berhane Selassie (meaning: Light of the Trinity – Marley had taken the new name when he was accepted into the Ethiopian Orthodox Church, in New York shortly before he died), lay in state at the National Arena, a huge concrete gymnasium originally built for the British Commonwealth Games. The lines of people queuing extended in serpentine pleats along the length of the building, and every so often there'd be a scampering as a line grew unruly and the police ran in spraying tear gas. Youths, all ready in their running shoes, shrunken grannies, groups of corn-rowed schoolgirls, the hotel hookers – all pell-melled away from the advance. But the people kept coming back, eyes streaming, shouting to the police about how Babylon (the Western capitalist society that has engulfed even Africa also, the police), must learn to respect the Dread.

The lines were orderly again now, no more tear gas, and the people would wait for hours to file through the high grey assembly hall, be-ribboned with red, green and gold pennants, hung with Wailers stage backdrops of Selassie and Marcus Garvey, and dotted with Biblical texts:

"Joseph is a fruitful bough, even a fruitful bough by a well whose branches run over the well. The archers have sorely quivered him, and shot him, and hated him . . ." (*Genesis 49, v.22–23*)

Marley lay surrounded by the same policemen he'd spent much of his life avoiding. You could tell he'd been flown in from Miami because the embalmers had refined an antiseptic film-star cleanness of line that Marley's living spirit had always blurred with motion. Cased behind glass, resembling a waxworks image, the lying-in underlined the fact that the corpse was a house for the spirit, and that the house had been locked up. Owner gone away.

Cedella Booker, Bob Marley's mother.

Rita Marley.

Tape loops of Wailers music played continually. People couldn't help but sing and dance as they passed the coffin. *One good thing about music, When it hits, you feel no pain.*

After the private family service at the Ethiopian Church, the coffin was taken to the National Arena. The service was conducted in Amharic and Geez, African languages, as well as English. Pleas to Jesus were countered with cries of "Jah! Rastafari" from conflicting churches. The politicians Marley had castigated so often gave tribute.

Odd, in this fluorescent municipal setting, to hear the reedy call-to-prayer chants you'd associate with a mosque; to see the priests shimmer in elaborate brocade robes beneath fringed umbrellas, as if they were the Wise Men trekking across a daylight desert. Marley, temperamentally a peacemaker till circumstances didn't permit it, would have appreciated this blend of faiths and states.

The Wailers performed, with Junior Marvin gamely aiming to fill the focal gap. They played while Bob's mother, Cedella Booker, sang a gospel chorus. Unused to the microphone, her voice kept vanishing. The previous night, rehearsing at the Tuff Gong studios, her voice had been astonishingly sonorous, heavy with lament. Ziggy and Stevie, two of Marley's sons, strutted and leaped on stage (a combo of junior Marleys called the Melody Makers were Bob's joy – he'd been writing songs for them for years). The I Threes sang with wrenching passion the 'Rastaman Chant': *One bright morning, when my work is over, I will fly away home . . .*

Marley took his friends back to his roots for the interment. The massive motorcade re-traced his passage from the country to Kingston. Washington Boulevard is one of the city's main exits – a long, bleached-out avenue that crosses deep gullies (draining ditches), lined with a mosaic of colour – walls of rusty zinc squares, corrugated iron, bright painted bamboo, lurid painted signs on shack shops. Now it's re-named Bob Marley Boulevard. Ahead, a sound-system truck blared Marley music as the procession moved through lukewarm rainy-season showers till the sun came out again. The streets were crammed with crowds, more than a market day. The emotion was almost physical; for days, people had been singing Marley songs to themselves, now they were singing in unison.

Reaching the valley of Nine Miles, Bob's birthplace, was as difficult as approaching a pop festival. There were so many Twelve Tribes Dreads dressed in white and the blood, soil, growth colours of Ethiopia that the ram-packed hillsides looked like a kinetic field of poppies and daisies. Peter Tosh and Bunny Wailers did not attend. Bunny is vehemently anti-funeral, (though this gathering was a life celebration), and Peter had horrified Kingstonians by saying on the radio that Marley had peaked when he, Peter, had been supplying 'decoration' as a Wailer.

There was one reunion: despite former friction, the Wailers' ex-manager, Don Taylor's strong arm supported the bereaved family publicly.

The National Arena.

Ziggy Marley, Bob's eldest son.

Marley's son Stevie.

The way the tomb was constructed, rough-hewn, gave it the air of an Egyptian shrine. Its low rise is feet away from a basic wooden two-room shack painted red, green and gold; rough-edged logs overlap on the walls, and small squares of window frame lush vegetation. Here, says Rita Marley, splashing a sudden smile, she spent the six happiest years of her life, with Bob. Here their eldest child, Ziggy was born. This monument is on the spot where they always used to sit out and reason under the tree, tracing the blazing stars, listening to the tape-loop of screeching, hooting night insects. A hundred yards away, Bob's mother was born. Clustered tight all round is Bob's family, who still remember him filching fruit to sell as a lively youth.

Before Rita had smoothed the Jamaican flag over her husband's casket, with the extra affectionate pat of a mother tucking in her child, she'd placed a twig of ganja inside. He would be smoking now, watching with amusement perhaps, the plans of the government to reinforce their Order of Merit medal with a special statue in a new National Heroes park; the authorities hadn't always given him such respect. He would be listening to the Wailers' plans to continue, using original material by all the members but structuring the team differently, now that the Skipper wasn't around.

Rita said that after all the pain, it was better that Bob should be at rest here in Nine Miles where he'd been happy. One thing she was sure of. "The works *will* continue."

Edward Seaga.

Nine Miles in St. Ann's, Marley's birthplace.

Nine Miles in St. Ann's, Marley's birthplace.

DISCOGRAPHY

SINGLES

BLUE MOUNTAIN:
Baby We've Got A Date/Stop That Train
BULLET:
Soultown/Let The Sun Shine On Me
Lick Samba/Samba (*Beverleys*)
CBS:
Reggae On Broadway/Oh Lord I Got To Get There
CLOCKTOWER:
Duppy Conqueror/Duppy Version
COXSONE:
Dancing Time/Treat Me Good (*Peter Touch & The Wailers*)
Rudie/Rudie Part Two (*Bob Marley and a Studio One band*)
I'm Still Waiting/Ska Jerk
DOCTOR BIRD:
Rude Boy/Ringo's Theme (This Boy) (*B-side: Roland Alphonso And The Soul Brothers*)
Nice Time/Hypocrite
Good Good Rudie/Oceans 11 (*B-side: The City Slickers*)
Rasta Put It On/Ska With Ringo (*A-side: Peter Touch & The Wailers; B-side: Roland Alphonso*)
ESCORT:
To The Rescue/Run For Cover
GREEN DOOR:
Trenchtown Rock/Grooving Kingdom
Lively Up Yourself/Live: Tommy McCook (*produced by Marley*)
Guava Jelly/Redder Than Red (*produced by Marley*)
ISLAND:
Judge Not/Do You Still Love Me
One Cup Of Coffee/Judge Not (*B-side: The Skatalites*)
One Cup Of Coffee/Exodus (*B-side: Ernest Ranglin*)
It Hurts To Be Alone/Mr. Talkative
Playboy/Your Love
Hoot Nanny Hoot/Do You Remember (*Peter Touch & The Wailers*)
Holligan/Maga Dog
Shame And Scandal/The Jerk (*Peter Touch & The Wailers*)
Don't Ever Leave Me/Donna
What's New Pussycat/What Will I Find
Independent Anniversary Ska (I Should Have Known Better)/Jumbie Jamboree (*A-side: The Skatalites*)
Put It On/Love Won't Be Mine
He Who Feels It Knows It/Sunday Morning
Rude Boy Get Bail (Let Him Go)/Sinner Man
Bend Down Low/Freedom Time
I Am The Toughest/No Faith (*A-side: Peter Touch; B-side: Marcia Griffiths*)
Concrete Jungle/Reincarnated Souls
Get Up Stand Up/Slave Driver
So Jah Seh/Natty Dread
No Woman No Cry/Kinky Reggae (*Live at The Lyceum*)
Jah Live/Concrete
Johnny Was (Woman Hang Your Head Down Low)/Cry To Me
Roots Rock Reggae/Stir It Up
Follow Fashion Monkey/Instr. (*U.S. release only*)
I Shot The Sheriff/Pass It On/Duppy Conqueror (*D.J. only*)
Exodus/Wait In Vain (*D.J. only – with Marley talking*)
Exodus/Instr.

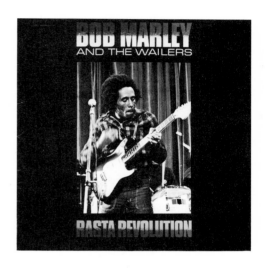

Waiting In Vain/Roots
Jamming/Punky Reggae Party
Is This Love/Crisis Version
Satisfy My Soul/Smile Jamaica
War/No More Trouble/Exodus (*Limited edition; taken from 'Babylon By Bus'*)
So Much Trouble/Instr.
Zimbabwe/Survival
Africa Unite/Wake Up And Live
Could You Be Loved/One Drop/Ride Natty Ride
3 Little Birds/Every Need Got An Ego To Feed
Redemption Song/Band Version
I Shot The Sheriff (*Live 12"*)
Stir It Up/Rat Race (*Live*)
Survival/Wake Up And Live
JACKPOT:
Mr. Chatterbox/Walk Through The World
PUNCH:
Small Axe/What A Confusion (*B-side: Dave Barker*)
Down Presser/Got The Tip (*B-side: Junior Byles*)
You Should Have Known Better
Screwface/Faceman
RIO:
Dancing Shoes/Don't Look Back
Pied Piper/It's Alright (*B-side: Rita Marley*)
You Lied/Crawfish (*A-side: Rita Marley; B-side: Soul Brothers*)
SKABEAT:
Simmer Down/I Don't Need Your Love
Train To Skaville/I Made A Mistake (*A-side: Soul Brothers*)
Love And Affection/Teenager In Love
And I Love Her/Do It Right
Lonesome Track/Zimmerman
Lonesome Feelings/There She Goes
SMASH:
Stop The Train/Caution
Freedom Train
SUMMIT:
Stop The Train/Caution (*Beverleys*)
TROJAN:
Stir It Up/This Train
Soul Shakedown Party/Shakedown Version
But I Do/Your Love
Soul Shakedown Party/Caution
Mr. Brown/Trenchtown Rock
TUFF GONG:
Lick Samba/Samba
Rat Race/Part Two
Smile Jamaica Parts One And Two
Work/Guided Missile (*Produced by A. Barrett*)
Roots Rock Reggae/War
Exodus/Instr.
A Jah Jah/Jah Version (*Bob and Rita Marley*)
Rastaman Live Up/Don't Give Up
Blackman Redemption/Version
Hypocrite/Nice Time
Ambush/Ambush In Dub
One Drop/One Dub
Comin' In From The Cold/Dubbin' In
Punky Reggae Party
Knotty Dread/Version
Craven Choke Puppy/Choke (*Wailers All Stars*)
Satisfy My Soul Jah Jah/Version (*The Wailers Group*)
Many Are Called (*The I Threes*)
Put It On (*Judy Mowatt*)